MAY 2017

SandCastle™

First Rhymes

The Cow
with a Plow

Anders Hanson

Consulting Editor, Diane Craig, M.A./Reading Specialist

ABDO
Publishing Company

Published by ABDO Publishing Company, 4940 Viking Drive, Edina, Minnesota 55435.

Printed in the United States.

Credits
Edited by: Pam Price
Curriculum Coordinator: Nancy Tuminelly
Cover and Interior Design and Production: Mighty Media
Photo Credits: AbleStock, Brand X Pictures, Anders Hanson, Hemera, Photodisc

Library of Congress Cataloging-in-Publication Data

Hanson, Anders, 1980-
    The cow with a plow / Anders Hanson.
        p. cm. -- (First rhymes)
    ISBN 1-59679-465-8 (hardcover)
    ISBN 1-59679-466-6 (paperback)
        1. English language--Rhyme--Juvenile literature. I. Series.
    PE1517.H355 2005
    808.1--dc22

                                                                    2005044263

SandCastle™ books are created by a professional team of educators, reading specialists, and content developers around five essential components that include phonemic awareness, phonics, vocabulary, text comprehension, and fluency. All books are written, reviewed, and leveled for guided reading and early intervention reading, and designed for use in shared, guided, and independent reading and writing activities to support a balanced approach to literacy instruction.

Let Us Know

After reading the book, SandCastle would like you to tell us your stories about reading. What is your favorite page? Was there something hard that you needed help with? Share the ups and downs of learning to read. We want to hear from you! To get posted on the ABDO Publishing Company Web site, send us e-mail at:

sandcastle@abdopub.com

SandCastle Level: Beginning

-ow

brow

chow

cow

plow

sow

This is my .

I see some .

We like the .

This is a .

I look at a .

Lara has bangs
over her brow.

The chow is good.

The cow is big.

The plow is yellow.

The sow is fat.

The Cow
with a Plow

Cassie is a cow.

Cassie the cow
loves to plow.

While on her plow,
Cassie the cow
sees something that
raises her brow.

From the plow,
Cassie the cow
sees her friend
Sallie the sow!

Cassie the cow
and Sallie the sow
drive the plow
to the mall
to get some chow.

About SandCastle™

A professional team of educators, reading specialists, and content developers created the SandCastle™ series to support young readers as they develop reading skills and strategies and increase their general knowledge. The SandCastle™ series has four levels that correspond to early literacy development in young children. The levels are provided to help teachers and parents select the appropriate books for young readers.

Emerging Readers
(no flags)

Beginning Readers
(1 flag)

Transitional Readers
(2 flags)

Fluent Readers
(3 flags)

These levels are meant only as a guide. All levels are subject to change.

To see a complete list of SandCastle™ books and other nonfiction titles from ABDO Publishing Company, visit www.abdopub.com or contact us at: 4940 Viking Drive, Edina, Minnesota 55435 • 1-800-800-1312 • fax: 1-952-831-1632